CW00968950

This book belongs to

Ena Manning
(Mc. Grath)

OTHER BOOKS BY CYRIL A. REILLY AND RENÉE TRAVIS REILLY

An Irish Blessing

I Am of Ireland

A Gift of

Irish Wisdom

&

Cyril A. Reilly

and

Renée Travis Reilly

Hearst Books / New York

Notice: Every effort has been made to locate the copyright owners of the material used in this book. Please let us know if an error has been made, and we will make any necessary changes in subsequent printings.

Copyright © 1995 by Cyril A. Reilly and Renée Travis Reilly

All rights reserved. No part of this book may be reproduced or utilized in any form or by any means, electronic or mechanical, including photocopying, recording, or by any information storage or retrieval system, without permission in writing from the Publisher. Inquiries should be addressed to Permissions Department, William Morrow and Company, Inc., 1350 Avenue of the Americas, New York, N.Y. 10019.

It is the policy of William Morrow and Company, Inc., and its imprints and affiliates, recognizing the importance of preserving what has been written, to print the books we publish on acid-free paper, and we exert our best efforts to that end.

Library of Congress Cataloging-in-Publication Data

A gift of Irish wisdom / [compiled by] Cyril A. Reilly and Renée
  Travis Reilly.
     p.   cm.
   ISBN 0–688–05292–4
   1. Quotations, Irish.   2. Ireland—Quotations, maxims, etc.
  I. Reilly, Cyril A., 1920–   .   II. Reilly, Renée Travis.
  PN6084.I6G54   1994
  082'.0899'162—dc20   94–20129
                                                              CIP

Printed in the United States of America

First Edition

1 2 3 4 5 6 7 8 9 10

BOOK DESIGN BY RICHARD ORIOLO

Acknowledgments

We thank the following for permission to reprint excerpts from material copyrighted or controlled by them. Every effort has been made to locate the copyright owners of the material used in this book. Please let us know if an error has been made, and we will make any necessary changes in subsequent printings.

Reprinted by permission of George Braziller, Inc.: "A Whisper About Bernard Shaw," *The Green Crow*, copyright © 1956 by Sean O'Casey.

Copyright © by Devin-Adair, Publishers, Inc., Old Greenwich, Conn. 06870. Permission granted to reprint from *1000 Years of Irish Poetry*, edited by Kathleen Hoagland, 1947, renewed 1975; all rights reserved: Anonymous, "Hospitality in Ancient Ireland"; Flann Fionn, "Alfrid's Itinerary Through Ireland"; Alice Milligan, "A Song of Freedom"; Arthur O'Shaughnessy, "Ode." Permission granted to reprint "The Plum Tree by the House" and "Lullaby," *Selected Poems: Oliver St. John Gogarty*, 1954; all rights reserved. Permission granted to reprint "Weep for Our Pride," *The Trusting and the Maimed and Other Short Stories*, James Plunkett, 1955; all rights reserved.

Reprinted by permission of The Goldsmith Press Limited, Newbridge, Co. Kildare, Ireland: Mairtín O Direáin, "Tacar Danta" ("Sturdy Oars"), *Selected Poems from the Goldsmith Press Limited*, copyright © 1984, 1992.

Reprinted by permission of H.M. Ireland: Denis Ireland, "From the Irish Shore," copyright © H.M. Ireland (n.d.).

Reproduced with permission, from *The Irish Times*: Rev. Michael MacGreil, "This Week They Said," May 15, 1971.

Reprinted by permission of Tom MacIntyre, "A Glance Will Tell You and a Dream Confirm," copyright © 1992.

Reprinted by permission of Macmillan London Ltd.: *Drums Under the Windows* by Sean O'Casey, copyright 1946; *Purple Dust* by Sean O'Casey, copyright © 1967.

Reprinted with permission of Macmillan Publishing Company from *The Collected Works of W. B. Yeats*, Vol. 1: *The Poems*, revised, edited by Richard J. Finneran: "He Wishes for the Cloths of Heaven" (New York: Macmillan, 1989); "The Municipal Gallery Revisited," copyright © 1940 by Georgie Yeats, renewed 1968 by Bertha Georgie Yeats, Michael Butler Yeats, and Anne Yeats; "A Prayer for Old Age," copyright © 1934 by Macmillan Publishing Company, renewed 1962 by Bertha Georgie Yeats; "Sailing to Byzantium," copyright © 1928 by Macmillan Publishing Company, renewed 1956 by Georgie Yeats.

Reprinted by permission of Martin Brian & O'Keeffe Ltd: Patrick Kavanagh, "The Great Hunger," *Collected Poems*, copyright © 1964.

Reprinted by permission of Oxford University Press: Peig Sayers, translated by Seamus Ennis, *An Old Woman's Reflections*, copyright © 1962.

Reprinted by permission of Random House, Inc., Vintage Books: J. M. Synge, *Riders to the Sea*, copyright © 1960.

Reprinted by permission of Routledge and Kegan Paul: Michael MacGowan, translated by Sean Ó hEachaidh, *The Hard Road to Klondike*, copyright © 1962.

Reprinted by permission of Russell & Volkening as agents for the author: A.E. (George William Russell), "Voices of the Stone" and "The Twilight of Earth," *Collected Poems*, copyright © 1925.

Reprinted by permission of St. Martin's Press, Inc., New York, N.Y.: Sean O'Casey, *Purple Dust*, from *Collected Plays*, Vol. 3, copyright © 1967.

Reprinted by permission of Sheed & Ward: Robert Farren, *This Man Was Ireland*, copyright © 1943.

Reprinted with permission of Simon & Schuster from *Drums Under the Windows* by Sean O'Casey. Copyright © 1945, 1946 by Sean O'Casey; renewed 1973, 1974 by Eileen O'Casey, Breon O'Casey, and Shivaun O'Casey.

Reprinted by permission of The Society of Authors, London, on behalf of the Bernard Shaw estate: "The Adventures of the Black Girl in Her Search for God," *The Portable Bernard Shaw* (Penguin), edited by Stanley Weintraub, copyright © 1947, 1977.

Reprinted by permission of A. P. Watt Ltd. on behalf of Bryan MacMahon: *Children of the Rainbow*, copyright © 1952.

Reprinted by permission of Wolfhound Press: *Proverbs and Sayings of Ireland*, edited by Sean Gaffney and Seamus Cashman, copyright © 1974.

Introduction

The world's fascination with Ireland is an undeniable fact. Those who know Ireland speak glowingly of its misty lakes and mountains; its green fields dotted with white sheep; its stone walls enclosing tiny plots of land; its prehistoric monuments; its ancient churches and castles; its villages with their houses painted all the colors of the rainbow; its magic place names, such as Donegal, Ballyshannon, Armagh,

Lisdoonvarna, and Skibbereen; and, encircling it all, its unfathomable, majestic, life-giving—and life-threatening—seas.

But those who know Ireland best are invariably fascinated most of all with its *people,* whose many-faceted, mysterious, highly individualized personalities intrigue at the same

time that they defy cataloging or labeling. Despite the impossibility of painting a complete and accurate portrait of the Irish, some of us nevertheless experience an irresistible urge to trumpet to the world at least something of what the Irish are like. In this book we have succumbed to that temptation.

But what *are* the Irish like? What should we say about them? Early on we decided to set the humblest of goals for ourselves: We would tell the world what *we* find most fascinating about the Irish. Over the years, we have talked with them in their homes and fields and pubs, read their poems (which, the poet Yeats reminds us, we must always do if we are to know the body and soul of a people), and absorbed their proverbs. As we talked and listened, read and pondered, a dominant impression began to emerge: Whatever else the Irish are (and they are many things else), they are a people brimming over with *wisdom*. In other words, as a people they seem to have an effortless grasp of the deepest meaning of life.

Not only that, but their wisdom is distinctively *Irish*. That Irish quality is evident not only in the areas of life that preoccupy them, but in their attitudes toward those areas. Above all, though, it is evident in the gifted *way* they express their thoughts and feelings: using language in which the words and turns of phrase are earthy, colorful, imaginative, full of surprise—unforgettable. In short, what the Irish utter at their best is wisdom elevated to the level of poetry.

Out of the vast body of Irish wisdom, we have selected for this book brief texts that in our opinion not only exemplify deep and abiding concerns of the Irish but also express them in a typically Irish way. Those concerns, and the order in which they appear here, are these:

- indifference to material possessions; importance of high ideals, a vision
- beauty and the arts of music and literature
- love of nature
- primacy of spiritual values and religion
- community, hospitality, friendship
- humor, laughter
- an independent approach to life
- patriotism and violence versus nonviolence
- old age, death, resurrection

Any attempt to convey what the Irish are like must present them in their natural setting—in the land that is as intimate an aspect of their being as breathing. It is not surprising that over the years we have both expressed and deepened our own attachment to Ireland by taking thousands of photos of the land and the people. For this book we have chosen photos that we believe give a unique visual resonance to the wisdom texts and that capture the spirit of Ireland. We hope you will enjoy the wedding of texts and photos.

—CYRIL A. REILLY

RENÉE TRAVIS REILLY

A Gift of
Irish Wisdom

The Ireland which we dreamed of would be the home of a people who value material wealth only as a basis of right living, of a people who were satisfied with frugal comfort and devoted their leisure to things of the spirit, . . . whose firesides would be forums for the wisdom of serene old age.

Eamon de Valera
St. Patrick's Day Address, 1943

It was better to walk without shoes and barefooted than to walk without dignity.

James (Kelly) Plunkett
"Weep for Our Pride"

O ur philosophy . . .
takes little account
of externals.

Denis Ireland
"From the Irish Shore"

Climb, traveller,
or stiffen slowly
on the plain.

Tom MacIntyre
"A Glance Will Tell You
and a Dream Confirm"

Your feet will bring you to
where your heart is.

Irish proverb

*C*herish the living coal

of your vision,

If you part with it,

you perish.

Mairtín O Direáin
"Sturdy Oars"

We are the music-makers,
   And we are the dreamers of dreams,
Wandering by lone sea-breakers,
   And sitting by desolate streams. . . .
Yet we are the movers and shakers
   Of the world for ever, it seems.

Arthur O'Shaughnessy
"Ode"

I have spread my dreams under your feet;
Tread softly because you tread on my dreams.

William Butler Yeats
"He Wishes for the Cloths of Heaven"

~

To know beauty one
must live with it.

Anonymous

~

A tune is more lasting than the song of the birds, and a word more lasting than the wealth of the world.

Irish proverb

The pen's trace remains though the
hand that held it dies.

Irish proverb

God guard me from those thoughts men think
In the mind alone;
He that sings a lasting song
Thinks in a marrow-bone. . . .

William Butler Yeats
"A Prayer for Old Age"

There is sweet music in the land, but not for th' deaf;
there is wisdom too, but it is not in a desk it is,
but out in th' hills, an' in the life of all things
rovin' round undher th' blue sky.

Sean O'Casey
Purple Dust

Very often I'd throw myself back in the green heather, resting. It wasn't for bone-laziness I'd do it, but for the beauty of the hills and the rumble of the waves that would be grieving down from me, in dark caves where the seals of the sea lived—those and the blue sky without a cloud travelling it, over me.

Peig Sayers
An Old Woman's Reflections

"The time I speak of, our lives were so thronged with small beauties that you wouldn't think 'twas sons an' daughters of the flesh we were, but children of the rainbow dwellin' always in the mornin' of the world!"

Bryan MacMahon
Children of the Rainbow

Leave me alone with my delight
To store up joy against the night. . . .

Oliver St. John Gogarty
"The Plum Tree by the House"

The best place to seek

God is in a garden.

You can dig for

him there.

George Bernard Shaw
"Adventures of the Black Girl"

The hidden light the spirit owns
If blown to flame would dim the stars. . . .

A.E. (George William Russell)
"The Twilight of Earth"

• • • • • • •

. . . the glowing, deep, unwavering eyes

Of those eternity makes wise.

A.E. (George William Russell)
"Voices of the Stone"

• • • • • • •

> ... **G**od is in the bits and pieces of Everyday—
> A kiss here and a laugh again, and sometimes tears. . . .
>
> *Patrick Kavanagh*
> The Great Hunger

The people . . . were as poor as could be. They had no land worth talking about and it was hard to make any kind of a living out of the little bits of soil between the rocks. But there was one gift the people had: there was friendship and charity among them; they helped one another in work and in trouble, in adversity and pain. . . .

Michael MacGowan
The Hard Road to Klondike

It is in the shelter of each other
that the people live.

Irish proverb

Who, being loved, is poor?

Oscar Wilde
A Woman of No Importance

*I*t's easy to halve the potato
where there's love.

Irish proverb

*I*t never was loving that emptied the heart,
nor giving that emptied the purse.

Anonymous

O King of Stars!
Whether my house
   be dark or bright,
Never shall it be closed
   against anyone,
Lest Christ close His
   house against me.

Anonymous, translated
by Kuno Meyer
"Hospitality in Ancient Ireland"

Live in my heart and
pay no rent.

Irish proverb

Think where man's glory most begins and ends
And say my glory was I had such friends.

William Butler Yeats
"The Municipal Gallery Revisited"

May the hinges of our friendship
never grow rusty.

Irish blessing

Two shorten the road.

Irish proverb

A friend's eye is a good mirror.

Irish proverb

We Irish . . . never hesitate to give a serious
thought the benefit and halo of a laugh.

Sean O'Casey
A Whisper About Bernard Shaw

Wherever the world is heading,
head the other way.

Michael MacGowan
The Hard Road to Klondike

The great appear
great because we are
on our knees: let us rise.

James Larkin
Speech to a labor group

Life springs from death and from the graves of patriot men and women spring living nations.

Patrick H. Pearse
Oration at graveside of O'Donovan Rossa,
August 1, 1911

Men do not prove their wisdom with spears.

Robert Farren
This Man Was Ireland

Wisdom . . . makes a poor man a king.

Irish proverb

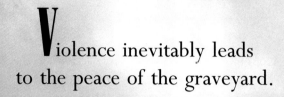

Violence inevitably leads
to the peace of the graveyard.

Rev. Michael MacGreil
The Irish Times, *May 15, 1971*

*Y*outh slips away as the water slips away
from the sand of the shore.

Peig Sayers
An Old Woman's Reflections

. . .*B*eauty that bloomed when youth was gone . . .

*Attributed to Flann Fionn,
translated by James Clarence Mangan
"Alfrid's Itinerary Through Ireland"*

An aged man is but a paltry thing,
A tattered coat upon a stick, unless
Soul clap its hands and sing. . . .

William Butler Yeats
'Sailing to Byzantium"

There is no King can rule the wind,
There is no fetter for the sea.

Alice Milligan
"Song of Freedom"

Bartley will have a fine
coffin out of the white
pine boards, and a deep
grave surely. What more
can we want than that?
No man at all can be
living forever, and we
must be satisfied.

John Millington Synge
Riders to the Sea

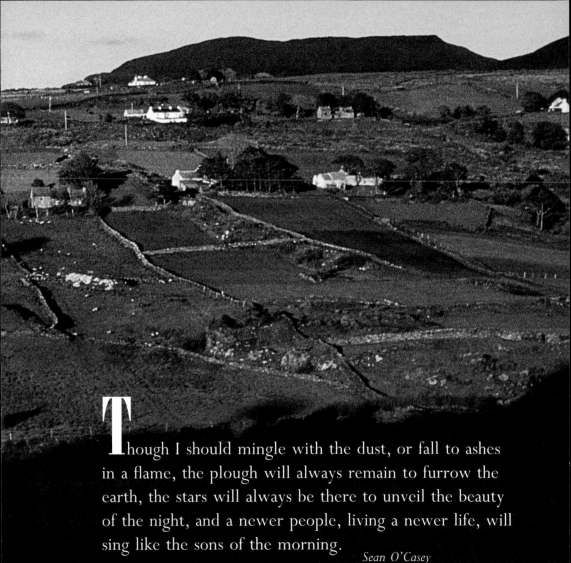

Though I should mingle with the dust, or fall to ashes in a flame, the plough will always remain to furrow the earth, the stars will always be there to unveil the beauty of the night, and a newer people, living a newer life, will sing like the sons of the morning.

Sean O'Casey

. . . So yield to dream.

Oliver St. John Gogarty
"Lullaby"

Locations of Special Interest